I0756645

Trumpism: Winter in America

(or, A Fascist Chronicle)

**Copyright 2020
Ron Jacobs**

Hanian Media

All essays were previously published in Counterpunch.

Thanks to everyone on the Counterpunch crew.

Dedicated to anti-fascists everywhere.

Donald Trump and his Trumpists are a logical result of US political and economic history. Trump is an almost perfect symbol for US greed, racism, and arrogance. His followers respond to his unwarranted sense of self importance and his easy ability to transfer blame for his actions and mistakes to others. They share his apparent belief that they have been wronged by those they consider lesser than themselves while taking little or no time to actually think about why the world they were living in no longer exists. Unlike Trump, many of his followers have no assets, little or no property and, most importantly, little power. Trump understands this on what appears to be a fundamental level despite his privileged upbringing. He is obviously not the first US politician to vocalize these sentiments to US voters, but his approach is certainly the most direct.

It is always important to remember when considering Trumpism that Trump did not win the popular vote in 2016. If the United States did not have the essentially white supremacist Electoral College, Donald Trump would not be in the White House. As many readers already know, this is part of the reason the founding fathers instituted this system: to keep rich white men in power. One can argue if they could have foretold someone like Donald Trump, but the truth is Andrew Jackson won the presidency a century before Trump did.

Ultimately, however, it doesn't matter that Trump did not win the popular vote. He is in the White House and he has done much to recreate the US government. This remaking of the government has made it less democratic, less fair, and considerably more remote. Pretenses that existed under the three previous regimes have been dropped. The government is not just complicit in the transfer of wealth from the working classes to the wealthiest, it is now leading the charge via massive tax cuts for the richest residents, deep cuts to public services for veterans, the poor, and working people among others, intentionally understaffing agencies so they will fail in their assigned missions, and massive privatization of public holdings and services. Those are just the most obvious elements of the Trumpist coup. Other aspects of Trumpism are less about capitalism and more about white supremacy and racial hatred. It is this combination of factors that lead me to label Trumpism as a US fascist movement.

I wrote the essays in this collection beginning in 2016 as the Trump campaign hit the ground. They are arranged chronologically and are an attempt to chronicle through my eyes the assimilation of Trumpism into the US body politic. Given the publication date, it's clear this story is not over.

I think some people started paying attention. I also believe the ruling elites are fighting among themselves for control. Clinton/Bush/Obama were all members more or less of the same faction while Trump represents another faction. My biggest concern with Trump is his equating working for the government to be working for him. Nixon was like that. He got taken down by opposing factions. One difference between now and Nixon time is FoxNews and the rightwing media machine. It existed back in the 1970s, but the media was not owned by so few entities and none were as powerful as Fox is now, not even the Times or the Post on the liberal side of things.

Or, that there's almost no veneer of decency and good intentions put on top of the corruption, nor attempts to hide the indefensible things. A good example is Paul Manafort who was basically allowed to do his thing for 35 years, and all of a sudden is now getting investigated and indicted. Did he suddenly become a bad guy? Are we to believe that he didn't do illegal things while lobbying for dictators his entire career before 2016? He didn't take any blood money? Or did something else change...

As for the Trump and Russia stuff....I agree that certain so-called liberals are trying to make it seem like a new cold war. That is just ignorant for a number of reasons. Foremost is that Russia is as capitalist as the US is. Do I think Trump made some deals with certain extremely wealthy and probably shady Russian characters? Yes, because that's who he seems to do a lot of his business with. That is where the undue influence comes into play. Some of those characters are probably part of the Russian government--like super capitalists in the US are part of the US government. Then again, maybe the Trumpists are hoping to reorganize imperial alliances along different lines—Russia, US, Brazil and other rightist nations as the new Axis?

I personally think Trump is the perfect poster boy for the downhill spiral these United States is in.......he's venal, crooked, somewhat stupid and not very aware of how he looks to the rest of the world (or maybe just to fricking arrogant to care). As I write this, the streets of towns and cities across the United States are filled with protesters demanding racial, economic and social justice. These protests were sparked by another blatant murder of an unarmed Black man by police. In a time when a pandemic kept much of the nation in quarantine and in the process exposed the true misanthropic and hateful nature of US capitalism. The nine minute video showing a cop slowly killing a human being by kneeling on his neck while other cops helped him by preventing any help from assisting the dying man was the catalyst that set off the largest social rebellion in the United States since the period we call the Sixties. Authorities across the nation answered the protests with brutal police attacks. Donald Trump and his cabal are demanding the military take over, claiming the brutality of the police is too "weak."

Trumpists are as convinced as Trump himself that the liberal establishment has it in for Trump and will stop at nothing to end his presidency. Besides the fact that this paranoia is mostly unwarranted (at least as far as the majority of establishment liberals is concerned), there is something else going on here.

In short, this is part of an ongoing attempt to remove the final sets of checks and balances in the US government. Already, the Congress and the courts are under the control of a relatively small group of super wealthy rightwingers and those who serve them. If the Trumpists are able to gain control of the various national intelligence agencies, the government will end as we know it. In its place will be a regime solely in the hands of those best represented by the ultraright John Birch Society and the Federalists. It is the latter organization that groomed Kavanaugh for the Supreme Court. He and others in the court system and elsewhere throughout the US government are gearing up for nothing short of a coup.

Mein Trumpf Makes a Stop in Burlington, Vermont

Thankfully, the temperature in Vermont on Thursday January 7th, 2016 was warmer than the single digit weather that greeted the earlier part of the week. Sure, it was only around freezing, but in Vermont that's a warm winter day.

The center of Burlington, Vermont's downtown is a six or seven block pedestrian mall with cross streets. The pedestrian mall runs north to south and is named Church Street (a common street name in New England towns.) When my buddy and I got off the city bus at the north end of Church Street, a small crowd of union members and anarchists was gathering. I spoke with a few friends in the crowd before we headed south to the other end of the pedestrian mall. This is where the Flynn Theatre is. That is the venue Trump spoke at. The street the theatre is on—Main Street—was closed off for a block with police cars and barricades. The barricades also ran down both sides of the street, meaning the street itself was empty in that block except for numerous police from various agencies. The anti-Trump protesters were kept on the north side of the barricades, while the people hoping to get into the Trump event were on the south side. At this time the protester number perhaps 200; the line for the Trump attendees was about 2000. After fifteen minutes or so, my buddy went to get a cup of coffee and I headed back up to the top of Church Street. The crowd there had grown to about one hundred. We marched down the pedestrian mall, with many folks chanting anti-Trump and anti-fascist slogans. It took perhaps twenty-five minutes to meet up with the crowd at the south end of the mall opposite the Flynn Theatre. Our arrival swelled the growing crowd to around five hundred.

As the afternoon turned into evening, the temperature dropped below freezing, the protesting crowd continued to grow and the Trump supporters grew more boisterous. By 6 PM, the anti-Trump crowd was well over a thousand in number. Their chants were loud and referenced Trump's racism and sexism, while also supporting immigrants and refugees. Across the street, Trump supporters responded with a couple oldies but goodies of the right wing crowd: "USA!USA! and "Get a Job!" Burlington city officials looked out of their offices in City Hall where a large hand-lettered sign in the windows read "Refugees welcome here." The two crowds were substantially different in makeup. The protesters were about equally mixed in terms of gender and their ages ranged from a large number of high school and college aged youth to many gray and white haired folks with a fair smattering of those in between. Although it was mostly white skinned (like Vermont) the numbers of African-Americans, Latino and Asian people was much larger than that of those waiting in the mostly white male line to see Trump. Indeed, there could have been ten non-white folks in the crowd of protesters and that would have been more than those waiting to see Trump. As it later turned out, at least two of the African-Americans waiting to see Trump got thrown out for protesting him.

Many of the protesters carried hand-made signs. Popular slogans were No Hate in my State and Love conquers hate. My favorite, though was the one that simply read, "Mein Trumpf." My favorite chant of the night was "Donald Trump you're a liar/We wanna set your wig on fire." When the line of those waiting to see Trump began to move, it became apparent that anyone wearing Bernie Sanders paraphernalia was being refused entrance. In addition, Trump security forces were questioning folks as to whether or not they supported Trump. If they answered in the negative, they were also tossed. Some of those not supporting Trump objected to this treatment and were threatened with arrest. Whether or not they would have been arrested was not tested. Despite these precautions by Trump's brownshirts, a couple dozen anti-Trump supporters got in. Most got tossed over the course of the speech when they heckled the lout. After leaving, several indicated that the theatre was not completely full, despite Trump's campaign giving away 20,000 tickets online.

Outside, the crowd fluctuated in size. I would guess that at its peak there were more than a thousand people protesting Trump's presence. Many held candles, some chanted and shouted, some played music and danced, while most hung out in the cold, talking it up with others, occasionally joining in on the chants or the dancing, and enjoying the scene. A socialist friend of mine called it a festival of protest. I thought he described it perfectly. By 8:00 PM, the crowd was beginning to dwindle. I had to catch a bus and left the area around 8:30 PM. There were still several hundred protesters.

As I walked away, I noticed a young woman arguing with the father of a young girl on the crowd's edge. The girl, who looked about twelve or thirteen, was holding a handwritten Trump sign. The father said he supported Trump because he was afraid for his daughter. ISIS and criminal migrants topped his list of fears. The young woman argued that she thought respect for other people's religion and ethnicity was a better way to fight fear than the hatred Trump identifies with. The argument was spirited but not threatening to either of the young females. The crowd was chanting "Another world is possible" to the beat of a snare drum. There was a group of high school girls on the bus making fun of a guy wearing a Trump button who told them he was a nazi. This happened while they were standing in line to get in to the speech. When they got to the front of the line, they were asked if they supported Trump. They said no and were told they could not enter.

In our celebrity focused culture, getting people to focus on Trump's politics and not his loutish behavior is a challenge, even among leftists. The discussions prior to the protests in Burlington included the suggestion to just ignore him. After all, we are told that he hates being ignored. While that might seem to make sense, I found it necessary to remind folks that one cannot ignore his politics. Instead, they must be challenged in every arena possible, including on the streets of every town he decides to speak in. Ignoring a wannabe fascist can easily be seen as weakness, not strength. These types of moral protest assume that people like Trump might actually have doubts as to the correctness of their views. The truth is, they don't.

The Trump campaign reminds me of other campaigns I have observed in my lifetime: Ronald Reagan, the George Bush's, and Richard Nixon's. However, the one it most closely resembles is the 1968 and 1972 campaigns of Alabama's George Wallace. Both campaigns were racist to the core and played on the fear of the working class white fear of a Black nation. His contempt for what he called the pinheads in DC was merely a cover for the anger southern white racists felt for the recent spate of laws passed by the federal government making racial segregation illegal. Despite the fact that the white power structure is still in command in the US South, along with the rest of the nation, politicians like Wallace and Trump know that they can manipulate white US residents' fear of the Other to their advantage. Although Trump is not as overtly racist when it comes to African-Americans as Wallace was, this is only because he knows it wouldn't play as well as it did fifty years ago. However, believe me, many of his supporters, advisors and donors are just as racist as Wallace's were, if not more so. In order to hook in more mainstream voters, however, Trump plays on more current fears: Latin American immigrants and Muslims. By playing on these fears, Trump and his campaign can bring folks who might otherwise be turned off by the support he receives from nazis, klansmen and other white supremacist into his protofascist campaign, thereby opening these Middle Americans to the extremist politics of those extremist supporters.

A Scheme is Not a Vision

I've attended counter-inaugural protests against Nixon (in Frankfurt, Germany), Reagan, Bush the Elder and Dubya. I found the experience to be cathartic each time, but not very long-lasting in terms of actual social change. Still, I think it was time well spent. I was originally planning to attend the protests against Trump and his right wing minions, but family stuff came up and I did not. In a way, I am glad since I might well have been one of the couple hundred charged with felony riot charges. It's not that I necessarily support the tactics of the Black Bloc, but I tend to find myself where the action is in such situations, especially when the alternative is listening to speeches and dealing with parade marshals, liberals and paper sellers. The fact that the charges against those arrested--those whose strategy is to make the US ungovernable or at least be a major pain in the ass to the new authoritarian regime--are felony charges seems to bode ill for unpermitted protests the next four years. It's not that unpermitted protests were treated much better under Obama; it's just that with the Trumpists in power there are certain to be a lot more protests and law enforcement much more willing to beat the shit out of people protesting. When the State is desperate it always resorts to force.

As Trump holds meetings with corporate America and promises to get rid of health, labor and safety regulations and impose protective tariffs on US products made elsewhere, the drool from the CEO faction floods the meeting room while they count the profits they hope to make. "We like what we hear" is the summation of corporate America's boardrooms. Of course, why wouldn't they? Their minimal allegiance to US society is being curtailed even further by presidential fiat. More mansions for the few, more misery for the many. In other words, a perfect capitalist state if you're one of the few who sit at the top of the economy. But, say some on the Left, Trump just tore up the Trans Pacific Partnership (TPP) trade agreement! That's a good thing, right? And, yes, of course it is. However, this action does not mean things will be better for US workers (even the native-born ones who fit Trumpism's definition of true American). What it does mean is that profits will be better for those who employ those workers. Nothing new there. Trump actually used the words "fair trade" when describing his reasons for ripping up the TPP. Of course, he doesn't mean fair trade in the same sense as those who sell coffee and other goods in food co-ops. No, he means "fair" for the corporations who hope to benefit. I am reminded of a three year old child whose idea of fairness includes only what is best for their self.

"At the bedrock of our politics will be a total allegiance to the United States of America…." For me, this line is the most alarming and most representative line from Trump's inauguration speech. Not only does it epitomize his idea of citizenship, it also seems to symbolize (along with his distaste for compromise) how he will deal with dissent. Sure, he prettied up this ultimately totalitarian thought with the requisite words about the diversity of the US population, blah blah blah, but the essence is simple. Allegiance to the State is the primary allegiance any resident of the United States should have. Any other allegiance is secondary. Those who share this allegiance with Donald Trump and his cadre are the "true Americans." All others are to be considered suspicious. I consider myself warned and ready.

In addition to that particular line, Trump's brief inaugural address revealed the world he and many of his followers live in. It is a world where public education and inner cities are jungles and where the world's most powerful military is weak. It is a world framed by a willful ignorance about the lives of others informed by fake reality television. It is a world where facts that don't fit this world are not facts and science is not real. Ignorance is celebrated and blame has replaced responsibility. It is a world that is a fertile ground for the likes of fascists and racists whose seed thrive in the gardens of ignorance and fear. Speaking of fascists, how about that neo-nazi getting sucker-punched? I have been asked my opinion about this action a few times. My first reaction was that of course he deserved it. Was it strategically a smart thing? Probably not, but nazis need to get what they deserve more often. Their politics are politics that need to be exposed, opposed and removed from the general conversation. The fact that such politics are even being discussed in a rational manner these days is symptomatic of the crisis capitalism is in. It is also an indication of the failure not only of liberalism, but of the Left's failure to organize a lasting opposition to capitalism and its ugliest spawn, fascism.

There is some hope, however. The size of the protests against Trump and Trumpism indicates the breadth of the opposition to Trump and his politics. The shallowness of the politics of that opposition's leadership indicates the work those to the left of the capitalist parties have left to do. If the bedrock of Trumpism is total allegiance to his version of the American state, the bedrock of our politics should be total opposition to Trumpism.

Making Torture Okay Again

Author Douglas Valentine has spent a good part of his adult life researching, investigating and writing about the US Central Intelligence Agency and its crimes. From his examination and detailing of the Phoenix Program in Vietnam to his most recent work titled *The CIA as Organized Crime*, Valentine has made it quite clear that torture is an oft-used tool in the Agency's toolbox. From the crude "wire to the testicles" approach in Vietnam to more sophisticated methods now called "enhanced interrogation," the CIA has led the way in American style torture of those it deems the enemy.

As most readers will recall, the years of George W. Bush's presidency saw an apparent increase in the use of torture by US forces—by both military and intelligence agencies. This increase was not only legitimized to the public and the press by some rather flimsy legal arguments, it was also defended by a number of elected representatives of the public in the US Congress. Among those elected representatives of the people was a certain Michael Pompeo, who hailed from Kansas. This man, who is on record defending US torturers as patriots while a congressman, is now the director of the CIA in Donald Trump's new regime. His appointment was supported by all but one member of the committee in charge of approving Pompeo's selection. The lone dissenter was the libertarian Rand Paul. In other words, members of the so-called opposition party (the Democrats) sitting on the committee agreed to the appointment, most likely taking Pompeo's false assurances that he would only use torture in specific cases.

I mention this appointment not because Trump's choice was out of character. One need only look at the rest of his choices for high ranking appointments to understand that the Trump government will be one of the most right-wing, self-serving, militaristic, and potentially fascist regimes to ever rule the United States. No, the reason I mention this appointment is because of the vote by the Democrats to approve a man who not only supports torture, but champions it. Now, I am not so naïve to believe that most of the rulers in Washington have any morals beyond that which makes them money or gives them more power, but to ignore torture (and thereby tacitly support it) is unconscionable. The fact that there is so little outcry around this appointment is one more element of proof as to the moral vacuum that is the US establishment. When combined with the other elements of what the regime calls the global war on terror—drone murders, Special Forces missions to kill and destroy, surveillance of everyone, etc.—it becomes clear that Washington has no right to claim any moral leadership of any sort. This truth is certain to become even greater as the Trump regime rolls out more and more of its executive orders without challenge from the legislative wing of that regime.

As I was writing this, a news item came across my desktop stating that Trump is going to issue an executive order lifting the ban on the use of "black site" prisons overseas in client states and nations occupied by US forces. This order overturns the order Obama invoked when he took power; an order that ended the use of such prisons by US military and intelligence forces. Black site prisons are utilized specifically for interrogation that involves torture because they provide a legal deniability on the part of Washington. One of the reasons given for reviving these torture chambers is that some of the people held and tortured by the US and its allies have returned to the battlefield. Let me remark (and yes I believe there is an element of equivalency here) that thousands of US troops returned to the battlefields of the "Global War on Terror" numerous times to fight and kill. Yet, they are not being tortured and detained for their actions.

Donald Trump is on record stating that he believes "torture works." I wonder exactly what this concept means. Does torture work for the torturer? Do they get the information they need or does it merely fulfill a need for revenge? In other words, are Trump and other who insist that torture works merely revealing that it is there psychological need to inflict pain on a perceived enemy? Is this what they mean when they say torture "works?" After all, most military experts disagree with those who say torture provides valuable information.

Author Valentine quotes Ed Murphy, a former operative in the Phoenix program, in his book on the operation. According to Murphy, "Phoenix was far worse than the things attributed to it." One can assume this is also the case in regards to the torture of detainees carried out since the events of 9-11. Indeed, the refusal by the Obama administration to release thousands of photographs taken in the torture chambers of Abu Gharaib suggest that the photos that were released are tame compared to those censored by the regime. The apparent acceptance of this censorship and the human rights abuses it is covering up is one more reason to call out the torturers and remove them from their chambers. It is also a prime reason to remove those who approve of these methods from their comfortable offices and positions. Failing to do so reflects on us all.

Trumpism's Gleichschaltung?

While discussing the current situation recently, a historian friend told me that he did not believe history repeated itself. Bearing that in mind, I asked him if he thought it still had lessons for us to draw on. He answered, yes of course. Keeping that under consideration, I decided to take a deeper look at the rapid changes Donald Trump and his "people" are trying to put in place in the United States. As I began my investigation, it was announced that Trump adviser Steven Bannon had replaced a General and an intelligence chief on the National Security Council. In essence, this move is another attempt by the Trump administration to upend the traditional chain of command (the professional class, if you will), with ideologues from outside that class.

Upon hearing of this move, I was immediately reminded of similar moves by Adolf Hitler at the beginning of his government. Now known as the Gleichschaltung, this time period in the rise of Nazism involved (among other things) the replacing of various members of the German government with Nazi ideologues whose primary allegiance was to Hitler and the philosophy of Nazism. Essentially the process of bringing all elements of power, from the government to the military to the trade unions to the media, into line with the Nazi state, the Gleichschaltung began with the elimination of independent state legislatures. This was followed by the dismantling of trade unions, attacks on the independence of the churches (especially those opposed to the Nazis), the elimination of all political parties except for the Nazi party, the creation of youth, worker and women's organizations where involvement was mandatory and enforced by the schools and community. In addition, the private militias of the Nazis became official state military organizations with the task of enforcing allegiance to the Hitler wing of the Nazi party. Crucial to all of this undertaking was the role of Hitler's right-hand man and propaganda minister, Josef Goebbels.

In the wake of the Trump administration's unconstitutional immigration order, the spontaneous protests and numerous lawsuits that took place in its wake, and the refusal of certain Justice Department officials to support or enforce the ban, and their subsequent dismissal, Trump dug in his heels. For many folks, the firing of the Justice Department officials was reminiscent of Richard Nixon's firing of officials charged with investigating his participation in the Watergate break-in and cover up (one result of which was the elevation of Robert Bork.) This became known as the Saturday Night Massacre and was but one of Nixon's authoritarian attempts to assume complete power of the US government.

Nixon's moves were eventually countered by the liberal wing of the US government. The result was his resignation. This saved the liberal republic that was the United States. Given the weakness of today's liberalism—and the fact that they are much closer in philosophy to the right wing than the Left—it seems unlikely that liberals will be able to stop the advance towards fascism we are currently witnessing.

Philosopher Ernst Traverso discussed in his most recent book the notion that the rise of fascism in Twentieth century Europe was partially due to the failures of liberalism; its economic failures, its rejection of the Left and accommodation of the Right, and its use of horrible violence to maintain its colonies and power at home. Those who argue that Trumpism is a direct result of the neoliberal capitalism prior to the US election of 2016 have that historical argument in their favor.

There is a trope that is appearing in various newspapers and in social media that focuses on the fact that Bannon has read Lenin. This fact is then used as proof that he is a Leninist. Nothing can be further from the truth. Liberal philosophy tends to equate communism with fascism in an attempt to make liberalism appear reasonable. As far as Bannon is concerned, a better comparison would be this: Steven Bannon is to Donald Trump what Josef Goebbels was to Hitler. Writing this is not meant to be alarmist. Instead, it is written so we can understand his role. It is clear from his work with Breitbart and in his production of propaganda films for the far-right that Breitbart is a clever propagandist. Indeed, it seems likely that he has read and absorbed Goebbels' admonitions and advice regarding the role of propaganda to the State. His appointment to the National Security Council is not appalling because it removes a couple of war criminals from positions they assumed were theirs by decree. It is appalling because it represents the rise of an American fascist to the inner circles of power. Not just the inner circles, but arguably a circle most fundamental in matters of life and death. Time will tell exactly what this means.

Another tendency among the liberal establishment is to discount the potential of the Trump-Bannon duo. This attitude assumes permanence to the US Constitution and its much-lauded systems of checks and balances. Furthermore, it also assumes a certain allegiance to that document and the system its words hold in place by those in power, no matter what party they belong to. This purposely naïve narrative ignores the ongoing reality in Washington. It is a reality that has seen the power of the president expand not just in arithmetic terms but in geometric ones the past couple of decades. What began with FDR during World War Two has continued under the auspices of national security, with the growing consolidation of presidential power drastically expanding since 9-11. If one adds the complete control of the Congress by a sycophantic and soulless Republican party marked only by an unparalleled and unprincipled lust for power and money all too willing to follow Trump's authoritarian march, the remnants of that constitution are in serious danger. There comes a time when liberalism (especially this current version) must put up or die the spineless death its actions have always solicited.

Where then, will the protest come from? The immediate response of people to the Trump administration's executive order regarding immigration seems to prove it will come from the people themselves. Although spontaneous in their actual manifestation, these protests are a result of numerous threads of organizing over the past decade—Occupy, Black Lives

Matter, antiwar agitator organizations like CodePink and even the Bernie Sanders campaign—combined with the efforts of established socialist organizations that maintain a constant presence on college campuses, some workplaces and at protests for social justice. While spontaneity has its benefits and the current protests have been quite useful in highlighting the unjust nature of the immigration order, there is definitely a need for an organized multifaceted resistance to the authoritarian state Trump and his associates seem intent on establishing.

The Deep State is the State

The deep state is not some enigmatic entity that operates outside the US government. It is the US state itself. Like all elements of that state, the so-called deep state exists to enforce the economic supremacy of US capitalism. It does so primarily via the secret domestic and international police forces like the FBI, CIA and other intelligence agencies. The operations of these agencies run the gamut from surveillance to propaganda to covert and overt military actions. This so-called deep state operates according to its own rules; rules which ultimately insure its continued existence and relevance. Although it can be argued that it was the 1950 National Security Directive known as NSC-68 along with the Congressional Bill creating the Central Intelligence Agency that launched the "deep state" as we understand it, a broader understanding of the "deep state" places its genesis perhaps a century prior to that date. In other words, a structure designed to maintain the economic and political domination of certain powerful US capitalists existed well back into the nineteenth century. However, the centralization of that power began in earnest in the years following World War Two.

For those who don't know what the NSC-68 actually was, it is essentially a directive that militarized the conflict between US capitalism and Soviet communism. It was based on the correct understanding that US capitalism required open access to the resources and markets of the entire planet and that the Soviet Union represented the greatest threat to that access. Not only did this mean the US military would grow in size, it also ensured that the power of the intelligence sector would expand both in terms of its reach and its budget. When one recalls that this period in US history was also a time when the FBI and the US Congress were going after leftists and progressives in the name of a certain right-wing ideological purity, the power of the US secret police becomes quite apparent.

As the 1950s turned into the 1960s, the so-called deep state's power continued to grow. Some of its better known manifestations include the failed attempt to invade revolutionary Cuba that became known as the Bay of Pigs, the use of psychoactive drugs on unsuspecting individuals as part of a mind control study, and numerous attempts to subvert governments considered anti-American. Among the latter actions one can include covert operations against the Vietnamese independence forces and the murder of the Congolese president Patrice Lumumba. In terms of the "deep state's" domestic operations, this period saw the intensification of spying on and disrupting various groups involved in the civil rights and antiwar organizing. Many elements of the domestic operation would become known as COINTELPRO and were directed by the FBI.

Although the agencies of the so-called deep state operate as part of the US state, this does not mean that those agencies are of one mind. Indeed, like any power structure, there are various factions represented. This means that there are disagreements over policies, priorities, direction, and personnel. The only certainty is that all of its members agree on the need to maintain the supremacy of US capital in the world. At times, the seemingly absolute power of the CIA and FBI have caused the US Executive Branch to try and set up other means and methods in order to circumvent that power. Two examples of this that come quickly to mind are the establishment of the Defense Intelligence Agency (DIA) by the Kennedy administration in 1961-1962 and the failed attempt (known as the Huston plan after its creator Tom Huston) by the Nixon White House to centralize the direction of all US government intelligence operations in the White House.

There is no soft coup taking place in DC. While the "deep state's" focus is always on the maintenance and expansion of US imperialism's reach, it is also a battleground where the conflicting elites of US capital compete for dominance. The entire government has been owned by big business and the banking industry for more than a century, if not since its inception. That ownership has been dominated by the military-industrial complex since about the same time as when the aforementioned agencies were created. That is no coincidence. However, their role in the current uproar over Russia and Michael Flynn is not because the "deep state" is taking over the government. It is because its current leadership represents the factions of the US establishment that were removed from power in November 2016.

Donald Trump is not against the so-called deep state. He is against it being used against himself and his cohorts. . In the world of capitalist power, the factions Trump represents are not necessarily the same factions represented by the presidents former FBI director

Comey served—the factions represented by Bush and Obama. Trump understands that if he can install individuals in key positions at the FBI, CIA, DHS and other security and military agencies, he and his allies will be more than happy to use the power of these agencies against their opponents. Indeed, he would most likely greatly enhance those agencies' power, making a further mockery of the US Constitution. If Trump is able to get the agencies of the deep state to work for the factions he represents—either by replacing those loyal to others not named Trump or by cajoling and coercing them to change their loyalty—he will think the deep state is a great thing. In this way he is no different than every other US president. He understands that whoever controls the deep state controls the US. The struggle we are witnessing between the FBI and the Trump White House is part of a power struggle between US power elites.

When the ruling class is in crisis, as it is now, the job of the left is not to choose one side or the other. Nor is it to accept the narrative provided by one or other faction of the rulers, especially when that narrative supports the police state. Instead, it is the Left's job to go to the root of the crisis and organize resistance to the ruling class itself.

Can NATO Still Make America Great?

Like so many other children of the Cold War, I grew up accepting the definition of the North Atlantic Treaty Organization (NATO) provided by the US government and its pliant media. In other words, I believed that NATO was a mutual defense treaty; a joint endeavor mutually agreed to by neighbors helping neighbors with a common goal of making the world better. According to this propaganda, NATO was created from a joint and equally shared desire to keep Europe free and democratic, just like we were told the United States was. The first time this understanding of NATO was challenged was when I attended a protest in Frankfurt am Main (where my father the Cold Warrior was stationed as part of the US military's NATO commitment) against the US war on the Vietnamese. A German college student with a protest sign handed me a leaflet written in German. Using my intermediate skills with the German language, I figured out that the writers of the leaflet considered US forces stationed in Germany to be occupation forces. This new perspective led me to begin reconsidering the nature of the military beast called NATO.

During his May 2017 state visit to several European nations Donald Trump managed to embarrass the US power elites with his boorish and ignorant behavior. Whether it was his rather bizarre photo session with the Pope or his appearing to shove the Macedonian minister out of the way during another such session, the establishment media wags could not express their embarrassment often enough. It appeared that Donald Trump was the modern personification of the so-called ugly American. In a culture driven by the obnoxious personality, Donald Trump was continuing his long-running act, only this time it was on a global stage and supposedly reflected on the rest of his fellow citizens. More interesting and potentially more historically important however, were Trump's series of contradictory messages about the future of NATO.

Foremost among those comments was this: "I said a long time ago that NATO had problems. Number one it was obsolete, because it was designed many, many years ago….We're supposed to protect countries. But a lot of these countries aren't paying what they're supposed to be paying, which I think is very unfair to the United States."

In one regard, Trump's statement echoes a fundamental misunderstanding of what NATO is now and of the fundamental reason it was originally created, both of which are the same yet manifested somewhat differently. *The American Interest*--a primarily neocon journal dedicated to projecting their version of what the interests of the US are--suggested in a January 2016 article that opponents of NATO included the following political views.

"First, there are those who support an active U.S. international security role but view NATO as obsolete, and even as an obstacle to building a more relevant alliance structure. Second, there are of course those on both the Right and the Left who, for different reasons, believe that the United States should pull back from its international commitments and global responsibilities. Third, there are hawkish internationalists who believe that NATO unnecessarily constrains U.S. international freedom of action."

If I were to place the Trumpists inside these categories, it would be a mix of those with isolationist tendencies and those who are hawkish internationalists. If one is to believe Trump's "America First" rhetoric, it would seem to locate Trump himself well within this latter group. After all, it's not like he thinks US forces should not be fighting wars around the world; it's more that he thinks US forces should be leading the charge and be able to invade, murder and occupy at will without any constraints from previous agreements reached by the United Nations or NATO.

Like the Monroe Doctrine written to declare US dominion over the western hemisphere, NATO is a child of the United States' self-manufactured belief in its specialness. That is, NATO is but one more spawn of the conceit of American exceptionalism. Coming into being around the same time as the United Nations and the Marshall Plan, the North Atlantic Treaty Organization was designed with the intention of projecting US military power in western Europe and as a bulwark against the Soviet Union—the other victor of World War Two. In 1948, when NATO was first established, only the Soviet Union had a chance at countering the tide of US imperialism. Any anticolonial movement in the former colonies of Washington's new allies was considered to be under Soviet influence. Consequently, that meant they were an enemy of the United States and its new alliance. Furthermore, other movements in non-colonial nations—like the Greek partisans fighting to overthrow the monarchy—were also considered part of the perceived Soviet drive to rule the world. In actuality, these movements were usually leftist and anti-imperialist, but not necessarily Soviet pawns. There was no way Washington and London were going to allow an anti-imperialist movement to sweep the planet, especially when Washington was planning on becoming the new imperial power. This is clear from both nations support for the royalist and fascist elements of the Greek civil war; some of which had actively supported the Nazis during World War Two. Further manifestations of this anti-communism were the various covert operations like those undertaken by the newly instituted Central Intelligence Agency (CIA) in the Italian election of 1947; elections which the communists would have otherwise won.

It may be difficult for some modern readers to understand just how deeply and intensely anti-communism informed the foreign and domestic policy of the United States after World War Two. Even comparing the current fear of "Islamic terrorism" with the anti-communism of the period in question fails to do the communist-phobia of that era in question justice. This fear of communism was institutionally driven by corporate America, which saw the appeal anti-capitalism might have on an exploited workforce. Driving the institutional fear were certain individuals: men like Richard Nixon, Joseph McCarthy, and John Foster and

Allen Dulles come immediately to mind. The inclusion of the Dulles brothers in this shortlist is directly related to NATO's construction as an anti-Soviet alliance. Even though career diplomat Dean Acheson is most often cited as a primary architect of NATO, it was the Dulles brothers who imprinted their anti-communist/anti-Soviet template on the organization.

Most of NATO's western press coverage from its inception until the early 1990s speaks of a mutual agreement by several western European nations, Canada, Britain and the United States to defend one another if one of them is attacked. As noted previously, any attack that might have taken place was assumed to come from the Soviet Union. After all, it was that nation which was the biggest threat to Washington's dreams of world hegemony. Even under this guise of mutual and equal commitment, however, it becomes clear that any defense was certain to be under the direction and command of the leaders in Washington DC and the Pentagon. This was apparent in the postwar arrangements in the command hierarchy that was established within the organization and in the nature of its funding. Another telling point was the denial of membership by the Soviet Union, which first suggested just such a move in 1955. Perhaps most telling was the alliance's insistence on opting for a nuclear defense instead of a conventional one. This meant that those nations with nuclear weapons would dominate the alliance; in other words, the United States and the United Kingdom would be in command. Of those two nations, it would be the US that sat at the top of the pyramid.

Despite the clearly imperialist intention and practice of NATO in its original incarnation, NATO's reinvention after the dissolution of the Soviet Union made that intention even clearer. Instead of searching for a way to end the mutual defense pact known as NATO, its leaders began searching for a new rationale for its continuation. After a speculative discussion in the media and various western legislatures in the immediate period following the end of the Soviet Union and Warsaw Pact, NATO leadership began to expand its reach. Newly autonomous nations of the former Soviet Union and member nations of the defunct Warsaw Pact were considered for inclusion in the organization. When eastern and western Germany reunified in 1990, NATO began its new envelopment of Europe in earnest. This was despite a well-publicized statement from US and German officials that there would be no further NATO expansion towards Russia's borders; a statement which was quickly ignored. It soon became obvious that the descendants of the Dulles brothers in Washington still considered the role of NATO to be the containment of Moscow, even if their ideological enemy was gone from that capital. In fact, the true nature of its purpose unveiled it as part of the machinery designed to prevent Russian influence from encroaching into Europe. Despite the eventual full-throttled turn to NATO expansion in the later 1990s, there were those in defense and diplomatic circles opposed to the move. Their main argument was that doing so would make Russia uneasy and possibly precipitate a new rivalry and consequent military buildup and arms race. Just like in 1955 when the Soviets suggested they be allowed to join the organization and were denied, it was the anti-Moscow element of the West's foreign policy establishment that once more decided a military rivalry with Moscow was preferred to some kind of agreement focused on making peace.

Another aspect of the post-Soviet expansion of NATO was graphically and bloodily displayed in the lands of the former Yugoslavia in spring 1999. After a series of demands from Washington and NATO that were considered ultimatums to surrender by the government of Serbia, NATO forces led by the United States began aerial bombardment of Serbian and Kosovar installations, towns and cities. This attack was part of a new mission for NATO; using its member militaries to attack enemies of the United States under the pretense of humanitarian intervention. Although the first such foray was inside Europe, the subsequent military actions took place in nations quite far from Brussels' NATO headquarters. The first was in Afghanistan, where NATO troops continue to occupy and fight in parts of the country. The second was in Libya, where a multisided war rages in the wake of the NATO removal of its leader, Muammar Gaddafi. All three of these engagements involved the murders of civilians and other non-combatants. All three of them met varying degrees of opposition from Moscow and Beijing, along with other nations.

Anti-imperialists and other opposed to NATO can dream that the Donald Trump White House will end

NATO. However, they would most likely be deluding themselves. Trump's criticism of NATO is centered on who pays for the maintenance of the militaries involved and the alliance's administration. His calls for greater contributions from other signees to the alliance do not indicate a lesser participation from the United States. Instead, they presume (and are a call for) an increase in military spending on the part of all nations involved. Given that the US defense industry remains a primary aspect of the US economy and if one accepts the argument that it is the defense industry that guides US foreign policy, the true motivation for this demand become clearer. Trump and those who think other NATO member nations should contribute more money and armaments to NATO are merely pimping for the defense industry—the machine that continues to play a major role in driving the US economy. If Trump gets his way, and every NATO member nation were to meet Trump's call for a 2 percent of their budget contribution, overall European defense spending would increase by $100 billion annually. If Trump and his administration want to get more than their share of that money, he can do little but encourage NATO to continue. Otherwise, the US share of those funds might shrink, with European and Chinese weapons manufacturers gaining the difference. Trump seems to have realized this fact and is acting accordingly.

Indeed, on July 6, 2017 the Associated Press reported that the Polish defense minister and Donald Trump had agreed to an eight billion dollar sale of Patriot missiles to Poland. The announcement, made the day before a state visit to Poland by Trump and two days before the G20 Summit in Hamburg, Germany, is an indication of the US defense industry's role in NATO's continued existence. An earlier agreement had already established an arms sale program that permitted NATO members to acquire and share US-made military hardware with other members of the alliance. This latter initiative, signed into being on January 30, 2015 under the Obama administration, is known as the SmartDefense program and was designed in large part to ensure that the US arms industry "remains a major player in the European defense market." (DefenseNews, 2/4/2105) As of late 2016, at least two NATO member nations—United Kingdom and Italy—were among the top thirteen purchasers of US manufactured armaments.

Donald Trump is known for making contradictory statements, often within the same speech. His remarks concerning NATO are no exception to this pattern. As I write this, Trump is in Poland to begin his second visit to Europe since his January 2017 inauguration. As noted in the opening of this article, Trump's first visit was marred by various controversies. Beyond the etiquette miscues and unusually boorish behavior in certain instances, there was Trump's failure to restate Washington's commitment to the mutual defense commitment stated in Article Five of the NATO Charter. This failure, intentional or not, set off alarm bells, especially amongst the liberal/neoconservative establishment, whose dependence on the status quo is what informs their entire political and economic existence. When stacked atop Trump's friendly comments during the campaign about Russia and its leader Vladimir Putin, what appeared to be his lackluster support for NATO stoked fears of a major realignment in the way the powerful run the world.

As if to allay those fears, one of the first things Trump said in Poland during his second European visit was quite explicit in this regard: "The United States has demonstrated not merely with words, but with its actions, that we stand firmly behind Article 5, the mutual defense commitment." In this same speech, he also echoed the neoliberal/neocon conceit that Russia needs to stop meddling in other nations' affairs. Among the nations he listed were at least a few that the United States has been "meddling" in for at least as long as Russia—Syria, Ukraine, and Iran. Essentially calling the US intervention in those nations a civilizing force, he called on Russia to join the US and other such "responsible nations" in their fight. Besides the disturbing appeal to some kind of western chauvinism, the expressed sentiment certainly sounds like a continuation of Washington's ongoing battle of words and intent with Moscow. Given this, it does not sound like much will change in terms of the historic relationship between these two capitals. Furthermore, if NATO is to be the projection of US power in the world and Russia is its primary opponent, then it would be pointless to fundamentally alter that.

Much is being made about the meeting between Trump and Putin at the G20 summit in Hamburg, Germany. While anti-imperialist, anti-fascist, pro-immigrant, and other protesters are attacked by heavily armed police outside the Red Zone created by security forces to keep the people away from the rulers of the capitalist world, those rulers discuss how to maintain their control. The contradictions of this endeavor are plenty, with different power blocs and individual nations vying for domination over the rest. While the United States continues to hold on to its role as the leading capitalist economy, the truth of the matter is that that hold is considered tenuous. However, it has minimal concern over losing its place as the largest and most lethal military power. NATO was one of the numerous means created to ensure this dynamic continued.

Despite the interconnectedness of the world capitalist economy, the nation-state is not dead. In fact, it seems to be experiencing a rebirth in this second decade of the twenty-first century. The Russian assertion of its territorial and national aspirations, the British exit from the European Union, the rise of nationalist political parties, and the occupancy of the US White House by "America-First" Donald Trump are all indicators of this. Donald Trump's campaign promise to "make America great again" certainly included the maintenance and expansion of the US Empire. This remains true no matter what his isolationist supporters might hope. That being so, the question then is not whether the US military will be stationed around the world, including in the NATO countries, but under what guise that presence will be maintained. Will NATO continue to be the military vehicle for the Empire in Europe and elsewhere or will Trump and his group of imperial bureaucrats come up with a different model to accomplish a similar end? In other words, will they re-invent the wheel if that wheel is still functioning how it was designed to function? No matter what happens—

and at this writing it looks like NATO will remain—
Washington's drive for world hegemony in Europe and
beyond will continue.

Trump and His Tariffs

If one looks for commentary regarding Donald Trump's recently imposed tariffs on steel and aluminum imports, they will find that most of those comments come from a Wall Street point of view. In other words, the remarks are concerned with how the tariffs will affect profits. A couple union executives have stated that the tariffs will be good for US jobs in the affected industries. In other words, steel and aluminum workers should have more work in the short term. However, other industries, like the automobile and canned goods industries, may suffer job loss because the costs of their materials will rise. This rise will mean the owners of said businesses will increase the cost to consumers. Since wages are pretty much stagnant across the United States, this will probably mean that fewer finished products made from steel and aluminum will be sold, which could very well cause layoffs in those industries, their suppliers and their sellers. This could in turn eventually result in layoffs in the steel and aluminum industries as well. In other words, the only sectors of the economy that can be certain to make money on this deal—at least in the short term—are a limited number of corporations and financiers. Even they cannot be certain.

Of course, some financial speculators have already started betting on the tariffs. In the days immediately following the tariff announcement, numerous news agencies reported that Carl Icahn, a billionaire investor and Trump's former special adviser to the president on regulatory reform, sold tens of millions of dollars of associated stock in the days preceding Trump's tariff announcement. While the sale may not have resulted in huge profits, the sale prior to the announcement meant that Icahn would not see his holdings plummet in value once the market reacted to the tariffs. Other speculators are most likely taking advantage of the dip in stock prices of those companies affected by the tariffs and buying them up. Once the prices began to rise, which they most likely will, those investors will reap the benefits.

Meanwhile, the working people of the US will probably never see any lasting economic benefits from these tariffs. Sure, some workers in the industry will feel that they have more job security; some may even see raises and many will probably get more overtime. Yet, those workers will not be immune to the rise in consumer prices, so the likelihood is they will not come out ahead very much if at all. These tariffs are not for the benefit of workers. They are an attempt by a faction of the US ruling class to squeeze more profit from a system in crisis; to internalize the neoliberal system as much as possible. The livelihoods of US working people are secondary at most in their list of concerns. Just as the system of capitalism is global in nature, so must the resistance to it be. When national governments present protectionist measures like tariffs as a solution to the problems working people face they are misleading the people. The only solutions to the problems facing working people around the world are those which are internationalist in their understanding and in their practice.

As a person who wants capitalism sent permanently to the dustbin, I have a feeling these tariffs could nudge the future in that direction. After all, the US is only one power in the world of global capitalism, and not always the strongest. Indeed, the imposition of tariffs could be a sign of weakness, not of strength. They could also backfire in ways quite dangerous not only to the general public, but also to Wall Street itself. Many pundits in recent days have brought up the 1930 Smoot-Hawley Act which imposed tariffs on 20,000 imported goods and provoked a trade war that exacerbated what became known as the Great Depression. Champions of the mythical free market (Milton Friedman among them) dispute(d) the idea that Smoot-Hawley had much effect on the depression at all, choosing to blame the Federal Reserve instead. The trade wars that ensued arguably led to World War Two. In actuality, the causes of the Great Depression were considerably deeper. The tariffs were a contributing factor but not the crucial element. Looking back, it is clear that the Depression was a drastic example of how capitalism works. Indeed, it was a market correction to top all market corrections.

Trumpists believe the current "free trade" deals like NAFTA are somehow unfair to US industry and banking. This is apparent in their attempt to exempt Canada and Mexico from the tariffs if they agree to certain changes in the current NAFTA. Although it is fairly clear that these trade agreements are harmful to workers around the world, the changes the Trumpists have in mind are not designed to improve the lot of workers. Like the "free trade" agreements themselves, the changes are primarily designed to improve the stock value of various corporations and financial houses. Working people around the world should be wary of those who claim that actions of the capitalist class are for their benefit. This is true when discussing the WTO and its gospel of "free trade"; it is just as true when the agreements made in the name of "free trade" are challenged or torn up by those in the capitalist class. When the Trumpists tore up the Trans Pacific Partnership (TPP) they did so because their ideas about maximizing profit for their friends on Wall Street didn't jibe with the ideas of those in the capitalist class who supported the agreement. While both factions tell the public that their approach to capitalist trade will benefit the public, they are only providing part of the story. Any benefits workers obtain in a capitalist economy are the result of struggle, not the gifts of the owners and financiers. Supporting the tariffs because of some imagined short term gain is merely buying into neoliberal capitalism's con game..

Nixon, Trump and Shadows on the Wall of History

Recently, the news storm around Trump, Putin, and the electoral shenanigans by friends and supporters of both men has reached a fever pitch. After Trump appeared with Putin in front of the media and said he believed Putin's denial of electoral meddling over the growing list of rumors emanating from intelligence agencies in the United States, liberals, some anti-Trump right wingers and most of the US media have been calling for Trump's head. According to this crowd, his remarks were treasonous and his continued presence in the White House is also treason. While listening to Democratic hack Steny Hoyer lambaste Trump and the GOP in a speech in Congress, various Democrats began chanting "USA!!USA!!" as if they were drunk Homer Simpsons at a World Cup game. The sheer foolishness of this action is beyond description. At the same time, it is to be expected in a political world where the shadow is perceived to be that which casts the shadow.

In other words, the collusion with Putin to destroy the USA is a sideshow, based on an ignorance of the manipulations behind the screen. Whether that ignorance is intentional or the result of decades of what I like to call People magazine personality-focused politics depends on who one talks to. Either way, it has created a situation where the political system in the United States that the public is presented is one where ruling class squabbles are not just the norm, but the predominant aspect of that system. While politicians on both sides of the aisle conspire to destroy not only any remaining social programs, but the economy itself just so they can enrich themselves, the voting public takes sides in a third-rate match between an insecure blowhard and con man and self-righteous liberals. The streets gain more residents everyday while multimillionaires and billionaires buy up property at rates so inflated they could support the economy of a small nation. Food assistance is cut and those who continue to need it are forced to work for the crumbs they are granted. Military veterans are watching their benefits shrink and the medical system designed to help them deal with their wounds of war get turned over to naturally crooked private enterprises designed to make a profit not heal soldiers. Cops around the country tout their military grade weapons when they arrest someone for failing to appear in court. More and more states allow concealed weapons to be owned by individuals, providing the trigger happy cops with an excuse to shoot those they don't like—who usually happen to be African-American and Latino.

I'm one of those who believes that history provides insight into the present. In my understanding, it is history that can help us understand the nature of imperial war and the reasons economies falter and fall. Most US residents seem to not just ignore history, but to deny it even exists. This arrogance, especially when considered along with the arrogance most recently displayed by those Democrats shouting "USA!!USA!" has helped to create the current situation. Not only has the regular citizenry fail to learn from the past, they have fallen prey to those who, having read and considered this history, have drawn only self-serving conclusions.

Why? Because they believe wtheir interpretation will keep them and their successors in power. This is why we have never-ending wars and occupation. It is why there is growing police state repression and surveillance. It is also why our economy is dependent on war and the preparation for war. It is also a primary reason why Donald Trump is in the White House.

Regarding history, let's remember Richard Nixon. On August 9, 2018, it will have been forty-four years since he resigned from the Presidency. It was his arrogance and egocentric certainty combined with paranoia that was his downfall. Before he finally got caught when his aides started squealing, Nixon was doing much more than covering up campaign corruption. He was running illegal surveillance that included break-ins and burglary. He was waging an illegal war on Cambodia and Laos. He ordered his Justice Department to set civil rights activists, radicals and progressives up on false charges in order to prosecute them and destroy the leadership of those movements. In essence, he was an authoritarian and autocrat. There were many times during his reign when many of us wondered if he was going to declare martial law. Then came the Watergate break-in and the newspaper investigation of the crime and growing cover-up. Nixon's paranoia increased and those closest to him began to scheme so they could save their own careers and, in some cases, their very hides. The Democrats, who were considerably more left-leaning then than they are now (or have been since then), saw their chance to jump. They did. Investigations began, including a special prosecutor's task force and congressional hearings to consider impeachment charges. The circus was on.

At its most fundamental, Watergate was a symptom of the empire in crisis. The faction of the ruling class that had almost always ruled the nation was fed up with the civil rights and Black liberation movements, the New Left and antiwar protesters, the counterculture, and social welfare programs. This faction, which Nixon represented, had always been working and plotting to take back "their" nation from the New Dealers and their successors. The other factions, of whom the pro-war Democrats were the largest segment, had enjoyed power for most of the previous forty years. Their social welfare programs were redistributing enough of the wealth to keep most people satisfied, but not all. Some of the nation's most wealthy resented the fact that their profits were being taxed and that money was being used to help many working class folks gain a stable life. As the Vietnam War continued and protests grew more popular, some Democratic politicians switched to an antiwar position. Newcomers got elected on an antiwar program. George McGovern even won the party's nomination for president, only to see the Democratic leadership sabotage his candidacy. When the news of a Watergate cover-up began to surface, all of Nixon's enemies from right to left eventually joined in the chorus. When the Republicans whose allegiance was not to Nixon but to the Party and their idea of the nation realized Nixon was toast, they joined his enemies. The resulting resignation was not a victory for the people or democracy. It was a victory for those who rule the plutocracy we call the United States of America.

The current circus around Trump and the 2016 electoral manipulation is also a symptom of a system in crisis. After years of war and ever-increasing income inequality, the Trumpists have drawn a line in the sand. If Trump is taken down it will be for his financial crimes and obstruction, just like Nixon was taken down for financial corruption and obstruction. Remember, Deep Throat was a disgruntled FBI agent named Mark Felt who worked with others in the ruling class to get rid of Nixon because Watergate was screwing things up for them. Felt had been intimately involved in numerous illegal activities as an FBI agent spying on and disrupting the New Left. He was no friend of progressive forces, yet his anger at not being promoted ended up serving the interests of those who opposed the police state he was a part of. This fact does not mean that what was leaked by Felt was not true or useful to those opposed to Nixon's rule. Nor does it mean the FBI and CIA are agencies worth supporting. These truths remain true today as surely as the CIA tortures people and the FBI spies on US residents.

As for Trump, chances are he will either get a majority of people in power on his side (most likely through firing current bureaucrats and hiring loyalists in their place), declare some version of martial law or get busted. If I were a betting man, I would put my money on the first option. These choices were Nixon's choices, too. This is a battle between factions of the ruling class. As the investigation continues, it is important to remember that the story in the media is not necessarily the actual story. If Trump is able to get enough of his people into leadership roles at the Department of Justice and at least one of the intelligence agencies, he and his faction will most likely win. Otherwise, who knows what will happen? Speculation is rampant, cheap and always changing. Keep your eyes on that which casts the shadow, not the shadow itself.

The American Dream Drives a Tank Down Pennsylvania Ave.

Andrew Jackson, Robert E. Lee, and James C. Calhoun are flying fighter planes over the Union's celebration of itself this Fourth of July. Jeremiah Jackson and General Custer are going after the Indians they didn't kill before. PT Barnum and the Amway company are celebrating that sucker born every minute with a huckster, cheat and liar named Donald Trump. He's a man with more power than all the money in the world can buy and his kids want to rent you a room in the family-owned hotel. The American dream is tearing up your neighborhood, taking over your television, installing viruses on your cellphone and promising you the moon. At least thirty-five million Americans are lining up on Main Street or sitting on their asses in some kind of air-conditioned comfort ready to be screwed in the name of freedom. Lee freaking Greenwood is shouting dime store patriotism from every speaker in America's hometown and even Uncle Sam wonders why God should bless the USA. What god would bless this unholy mess? What god would want to claim it as its own? Perhaps a dark lord from the depths of the eighth circle of hell? Lust, greed and gluttony define this American life. Its celebrated "freedoms" seem to revolve around guaranteeing these behaviors. Its current president has enshrined them in its house of whiteness. There is no shame.

Frat boys, yahoos from Mayberry towns, and rich men filled with hate and puffed up with empty egos push their agenda of white is right even though its wrong. The only stripes that really matter in the flag flown from Iwo Jima to Baghdad are the white ones. Black, brown and red-toned people have known this since the day they opened their eyes. The white-skinned folks who aren't celebrating this basic fact want to think it isn't so. Yet every time the line is drawn and they must choose where to stand, most of them white folks choose the side with the people wearing sheets and swinging axes like Lester Maddox. Old times there they aren't forgotten. Way down upon the Swannee river and all that. Look away, Dixieland. The legacy of the slavers informs this country more than any other legacy around. Let me tell you, it's great being white on Independence Day. A Klan member told me this so many years ago before my buddy told him to fuck off. Have a Budweiser and God bless the USA. Hell, have a bunch of Budweisers. And a shot of bourbon too.

Corporate America makes a killing. Corporate America is a killer. From the ICE raids in your hometown to the SEAL raids in Afghanistan and beyond using all the latest equipment manufactured and sold by everyone from Amazon to Apple, Wayfair to Lockheed, Raytheon to General Dynamics, corporate America kills and goes home to thousand-dollar bottles of Scotch and meals prepared by undocumented immigrants. Corporate America is America. Wall Street is controlled by small men with big egos and appetites for destruction. It is populated by smaller men and women willing to work for such men. Morality is defined by the ability to make a profit. Sociopathy is the name of the game. Human life is just a small part of their equation.

Holocausts and genocide are how they do business. If I
had a rocket launcher….

What to the slave is the Fourth of July? Slavery
abolitionist Frederick Douglass asked so many decades
ago. "The rich inheritance of justice, liberty, prosperity
and independence, bequeathed by your fathers, is shared
by you, not by me. The sunlight that brought light and
healing to you, has brought stripes and death to me."
Today, that sunlight remains a faint light to the humans
in the concentration camps set up by the immigration
police, to the descendants of those enslaved in this
country, to the indigenous peoples whose lands continue
to be stolen and to the poor. What to them is the Fourth
of July? A reminder that this country is not for them; a
reminder that this country only wants their blood, their
sweat, their money and, in times of war, their children.
Freedom, my ass.

Tanks driving up Pennsylvania Avenue is not
the definition of freedom. Overpriced death planes
doing tricks in the sky above the Reflecting Pool is not
justice for all. Donald Trump talking trash on the steps
of the Lincoln Memorial is not the Gettysburg Address.
However, it is this nation's bottom line, its ugly truth.
Its history of genocide and greed, war and lynching,
slavery and racism. The Trumpists have exposed what
really makes this country unique—its unadulterated
greed, its arrogant lies and brutal treatment of those in
the way of its greedy pursuit of gold. The Trumpists
have also exposed the myth of a liberal opposition—an
opposition defined by Pelosis, Clintons and Schumers
who know their interests lie with the Trumpists and their

legions of hate much more than with their pledges to justice for all.

America, go fuck yourself with your fireworks.

There Goes the Judge?

I don't trust judges. My experiences with those who sit above the rest of the courtroom wearing robes and assuming all will rise when they enter have rarely been positive and never worth repeating. The idea that another human whose primary difference from the rest of us is that they feel they have the knowledge, understanding and most of all the right to sit in judgment of others is one I have unwillingly acknowledged but never accepted. Like a confessor priest is to Catholics, the men and women on the bench dole out punishments and demand obedience from those who stand before them. Also like a Catholic confessor, the more arrogant among the judiciary probably think they too are doing the work of their god.

Me, I'm not buying it. From John Roberts to Earl Warren and Felix Frankfurter to the first Chief Justice John Jay, the judges in the highest court in the land are just as human as that lawyer advertising their personal injury business on TV. More than anything else, it is their ambition that got them to where they are now. Bob Dylan once sang that he was "ashamed to live in a land where justice was just a game." His words ring truer than ever these days, when cops walk free after murdering unarmed people and privileged white rapists are barely punished by judges whose understanding of the law all too often seems to depend on the wealth and social position of the defendant. Like virtually all those in powerful positions, many judges' sense of justice has been compromised probably more than once and their sense of duty has not always been to the principles they pontificate about, but to those who have helped them along their way.

All but one of my court appearances had to do with the possession of marijuana or my involvement in a protest. The sole exception involved a disturbing the peace charge that was eventually bargained down to a civil complaint over a noise ordinance. After the judge admonished me about playing music too loud, she gave me a ten dollar fine. As for the marijuana possession appearances, all but one of them resulted in me being sentenced to probation and community service. A friend who got busted with me one of the times had a different fate. While he stood on a platform surrounded by a mahogany rail in the Berkeley City Court and listened to the charge being read, the two cops who had busted him and me sat next to the prosecutor. The next part of the procedure would have the public defender enter my friend's plea. Instead, the judge looked over to the prosecutor and the cops and told the court he was dismissing the charges. To say the least, the cops and prosecutor were surprised. Before the prosecutor could respond, the judge looked at the cops and calmly called them out, stating that after reading the arrest report he had come to the conclusion that the arrest was illegal, without probable cause and stunk of police harassment. Furthermore, he continued, if they ever attempted to bring someone into his court under similar circumstances, he would bring contempt charges against the two police officers. Most of the courtroom could barely contain their glee as they watched the cops leave the courtroom. I wouldn't swear that they were embarrassed, but I'm certain they were pissed off. My charge was dropped. Justice had been served. Of course, after that episode my friend and I were on the cops' shit list and tread carefully whenever we saw them.

I tell this anecdote to make a point. Even if one doesn't believe the justice system in the United States is fair, it can make a difference who the judges are. Even though the system of justice in the United States is weighted towards those who pursue and protect profit, are white and male, a judge who leans towards the rights of the powerless and disenfranchised might keep a person out of jail. In the case of the Supreme Court, such a judge might bend the interpretation of the Constitution towards those without power in this nation. Their presence won't change the essential nature of the justice system, but it might make life a bit less difficult for those whom the power elites do not represent.

All of which brings me to Bret Kavanaugh. This man should never sit on any court, much less the Supreme Court. His judicial philosophy is informed by an elitist interpretation of the Constitution which is further reinforced by his elitist upbringing. His involvement in the torture of detainees under the Bush administration, the sexual assaults he is accused of and denies, the lying under oath in his earlier confirmation hearings—all of these are not just examples of one mans arrogance and self-righteousness. No they are symptomatic of the very nature of the system that grooms men and women to rule over the rest of us.

Bret Kavanaugh needs to be sent back to his suburban mansion without a job on the Supreme Court, thankful that he isn't disbarred. Ideally, he should be forced out of the entire judiciary and be relegated to chasing ambulances and buying tickets to Nationals games. I'm not holding my breath.

Refugees, A Hog Wallow, and the Midterms

While reading media descriptions of the migrant procession through Central America and Mexico two stories came to mind. The first is the song by Bob Marley and the Wailers titled "Exodus." The second is the flight of the Israelites from the Pharaoh's Egypt. When examined even just a little, neither the song or the biblical tale is a genuinely apt metaphor. However, the concept of a flight to a better place is suggested by both tales. In the song, Bob Marley sings "So we gonna walk - all right! - through de roads of creation...." and out of Babylon. In the instance of the migrant caravan, these walkers would seem to be walking towards Babylon (as in the United States—the modern Babylon.) As it relates to the biblical tale of Exodus, it seems fair to say that the procession is moving to the land of the Pharaoh (as in Trump). One assumes the hundreds in the procession feel differently, perhaps understanding their trek as a walk away from brutal and constant oppression and starvation. The future they face is uncertain, but it must provide a hope that does not exist in the places they have left.

The reaction of Trump, his advisers and the Trumpist media to the caravan—portraying it as a cover for "terrorists" and threatening the use of military force to prevent its entry into US territory—is more than just a mean-spirited manipulation of nativist fears. It is a morally reprehensible response to the plight of those Jesus would call the least of our brethren. In addition, threatening military action against mostly impoverished refugees is grossly inappropriate and most likely a violation of US law. Of course, in the world of 2018 USA, that means little. Moral reprehensibility and violation of the law are the modus operandi of the ruling party in Washington.

This nation called the United States is nothing more than a hog wallow composed mostly of manure. The larger hogs in the muck consume everything in their reach, their girth growing measurably wider with time. Occasionally these larger hogs fight among themselves, but only to determine how they will prevent others from getting any of the slop they gorge themselves on. The nature and breadth of their consumption is so grand it cannot help but mean they often consume their own waste. Oblivious or just not caring about the risks involved in such behaviors, the boss hogs step up their consumption. Those who wish to be like them—despite the enormous odds against that ever happening—mimic the boss hogs' behavior and defend them against those who do not share their passion for gluttony.

The brazen immorality of the nation's leadership is redefined as morality in newspapers, on television and in many of the nation's churches. Christians claiming to follow Christ and his two great commandments: Love the lord thy god and, secondly, Love your neighbor as yourself, seem to be full of self-hatred or confused as to who their god actually is. One can hear the more thoughtful among them asking themselves is my god money and the pursuit of money? Is it Donald Trump or some prosperity preacher? Do I hate refugees because I hate myself? To say the least, their churches are quite unhelpful in answering these questions. The New

Testament warnings against false prophets seem quite relevant. Conversely perhaps, so does Max Weber's observation that modern capitalism would create a society filled with "Specialists without spirit, sensualists without heart; {which} imagines that it has attained a level of civilization never before achieved."

Liberals look at their world, claiming to be mystified by what they see. Their struggle between doing what's morally right versus protecting the capitalist system has rendered them politically impotent. So quick to judge the faults of the unwashed, they refuse to meaningfully challenge the individuals determined to destroy them. As for the entities of power that once served them—the so-called deep state—liberals refuse to challenge the basis of these entities' existence—the pursuit of profit and the domination of the economic system—because it might mean an end to their bourgeois comfort. The crisis these liberals face is one of their own making. It is no longer only about holding power. It is now a moral crisis. One wonders if they will find the moral courage they have compromised to fight the proto-fascists now taking over the house they thought was theirs alone.

Recently, Donald Trump told his audience he is a nationalist. One wonders how long it will be before he tells that audience what everyone already knows: not only is he a nationalist, but he is a white nationalist. One also wonders how that statement will be received by the population. Will there be a flurry of sound and fury followed by acceptance of an proud white supremacist in the White House or will a genuine resistance to fascism finally be mounted? If it is to be the latter, then the

Trumpists must be stopped in their tracks now, beginning with the upcoming elections. Trump and his backers must be prevented from getting two more years to consolidate their power. Despite my distaste for liberal politicians, I plan on holding my nose and casting my vote for a few of them. After all, voting is just a tactic, not a moral position. In my mind, it is a tactic that needs to be employed this election cycle.

Impeach!

The midterm elections have concluded. The Democrats have regained the majority in the House of Representatives. One can be fairly certain that a number of those Democrats will begin to backpedal on their more progressive campaign statements in the coming weeks. After all, like their GOP counterparts, those backpedalers are primarily interested in their own future, not the future of those who voted for them, especially the voters with little or no money. Consequently, it is up to the voters who put these Democrats in power to turn up the pressure on these politicians and keep it up.

There is no better way to do so than to demand that an impeachment investigation begin against Donald Trump. His administration's abuse of power is at the least on par with that of the Nixon White House. Indeed, his Wednesday afternoon firing of Attorney General Sessions (who deserved to go for completely different reasons) and replacement with the Trump sycophant and scam artist Matt Whitaker is a page straight out of Nixon's script in 1973. Congress would be failing in its duty to the US Constitution and the American people if it does not begin the process. Ideally, the Special Prosecutor's office will provide any investigative committee with the evidence it has accumulated on the various criminal actions of Trump and his people. This evidence has already led to the convictions of numerous government and Trump campaign officials. One assumes it will lead to more. Trump's continuous attempts to intrude and block the investigation are just one example of his ongoing attempts to obstruct the course of justice. One can safely assume that his actions known and unknown in this growing scandal are enough to make him a co-conspirator. Whether or not he is indicted for being so does not remove the fact of his participation. In a historical sidenote, it seems important to recall that Congress did not want to begin impeachment hearings against Richard Nixon in 1973 but did so after overwhelming political pressure from their constituents.

Trump's criminality is assumed by a fair number of US residents. Judging from anecdotal evidence, it seems reasonable to conjecture that more than a quarter of US residents believe Trump to be guilty of at least a few felonies. Indeed, except for his hardcore followers, who have little if any use for the facts, it seems likely that of the millions of Americans who are withholding their judgement on Trump's guilt, many of them would have little problem with an impeachment investigation. Of course, there are much smaller numbers who believe any such thing will happen. This is primarily due to the overall perception that Congress does not have the guts to challenge Trump and his bully boys. This brings us back to why it is up to those US residents who oppose Trump to pressure Congress to impeach. The evidence must be heard by us all

In the weeks prior to the recent election, Trump used his powers as Commander in Chief to send thousands of US military forces to the southern border of the United States. According to Trump the reason for this mobilization—which is complete with helicopter gunships, humvees, airplanes, and a varied assortment of lethal weaponry—is the presence of a couple thousand refugees walking to the US border to seek asylum. Mainstream media have quoted numerous active and retired, named and unnamed US military officers stating that this mobilization is politically motivated, unneeded and an inappropriate use of US military forces. In other words, it is a gross abuse of the powers invested in the presidency. Trump's statements suggesting the troops will be allowed to use live fire on these refugees is a further abuse of those powers and, as far as international (if not national) military rules of engagement are concerned, completely illegal. The fact that the Pentagon has gone along with this abuse of presidential power, with some of its generals even using a convoluted rationale to justify it bodes ill for those who like to believe that the military will put the Constitution before the president. Indeed, "Mad Dog" Mattis appears to have already done so with these orders to send the troops to the US-Mexican border.

There are very few legislative avenues the elected representatives of the US people can take at this moment in history that might provide those who voted for them a chance to rein in the Trump administration. Cooperating with Trump and his right wing associates is not one of them. The election results make it fairly clear that the majority of the voters believe the Trumpist rampage needs to be stopped. The tax cuts for the rich must be repealed and the environment must be protected; the moves towards universal and affordable health care must be revived and the sheer criminality of this White House must be prosecuted. Any legislation supporting these ideas this Congress might pass would most likely be vetoed once it reached the Oval Office. Any legislation that is except for an impeachment investigation into the daily abuses of presidential power and the Trump administration's criminality. Trump has no say in that regard. This is reason enough to write letters and send emails to your Congressperson, organize protests, talk to the media and demand that a Congressional impeachment investigation begin. The time is now.

Presidential Papers

Donald Trump is a despicable human. This is a more or less common understanding among those who don't buy whatever he's selling. This being said, are you still wondering how Donald Trump and his followers "stole" your country? Are you still hoping you can win it back in the next election? Even more importantly, do you think it can be repaired if you do win it back? If so, what exactly do you mean by repaired? Does this mean you want it to return to those heady years under Barack Obama, when Wall Street took the nation's treasury and went on vacation? You remember, when the military budget continued to grow, the so-called global war on terror expanded to dozens more countries and the US used its drones to first kill suspected terrorists and their families, then launched more drones to kill the first responders who came to help them. Is that the nation you want back?

Or maybe it's the nation we lived in when George W. Bush was president; when Dick Cheney went quail hunting at a private reserve and shot somebody's face half-off—like the US military did several times a day in Iraq? Killing and maiming Iraqis for sport. You remember, when the planes hit the World Trade Center and the Pentagon and the PATRIOT Act—all thousands of its pages—suddenly appeared, just in time to save the very people whose class interests it served. The masses shed their tears for the dead in New York City, put on their red, white and blue underwear, rounded up the Muslims, and ate their freedom fries. Dubya told us to go shopping, the NFL paid for some GIs to march and noisy planes to fly while Major League Baseball made standing and singing the Irving Berlin pap called "God Bless America" a mandatory thing in the seventh inning every Sunday.

How about if we go back to Bill Clinton's presidency? That was some show, huh? Penis in an intern's mouth and prurient interest for the sanctimonious lawyer from Pepperdine—Ken Starr. It reminded me of the report on pornography back in the Reagan days; the report itself was at least as good as a poor man's Henry Miller. The only thing it lacked was Miller's writing ability and any imagination. Prudes have a hard time coming up with pornographic or erotic episodes. One assumes this is because their experience is limited to the most basic missionary activity. It's worse than their proselytizing for god, country and dollar. Clinton made the nation safe for Bush and Trump. It was his administration that decided poor single women with children didn't deserve a helping hand and openly called young black men predators. He made it okay for a certain wing of the Democratic Party to be openly racist again. Strom Thurmond died a satisfied man. The global war on terrorists that Washington doesn't need or want for its own purposes was ramped up under Slick Willie, but his dick-waving war crime remains the bombing of what used to be Yugoslavia. Made him presidential, they say.

I work at a public library these days. Last week a young man—maybe in his late twenties—began talking to a co-worker and me about George HW Bush. Dubya's daddy. He told me how Papa Bush was one of the best presidents in the history of the United States.

When I tried to point out that he was a CIA stooge and a corporate patsy, this fellow said but what about his work with the Nicaraguan revolutionaries? It took me a second before I realized he meant the contras. In other words, the counterrevolutionaries. I told the dude that Papa Bush was lucky he didn't go to jail for that criminal enterprise. Cocaine, guns, money and corruption. Classic CIA, classic criminality, classic anti-communism, classic gringo. The young man insisted I was wrong, pointed out that Ronald Reagan was probably the second-best president ever. What can you say? What is there to say? So, I asked him if he thought Nixon was the third best. His response was that Nixon was wronged by the commies and the Democrats. I told him that we did our best to get him out of the White House. The look of incredulity on his face was worth putting up with his right-wing history lesson.

I never understood the great communicator moniker the media gave to Reagan. I never understood how liberals could consider him a decent human being, even with them being liberals. During his 1984 re-election campaign Reagan made a campaign stop at a community college in Cupertino, California. Nowadays, that burg is in the heart of the concrete and ethernet jumble they call Silicon Valley. Back then, the internet egg was just being fertilized. The site of Reagan's campaign rally was a small sports stadium on the campus. Fences surrounded the entire facility. Cops, secret service and other law enforcement types flanked the two or three entry gates. Each and every attendee going through these gates was searched with a pat-down and a metal detector. I rode down with a couple carloads of people who were in CISPES (Committee in Solidarity with the People of El Salvador). Their plan was to unfurl their banners and signs and try to walk through the gates. Once they had gathered with signs and stuff they were surrounded by cops. Cops in uniforms, cops in shiny shoes and black suits, cops with navy polo shirts with FBI printed on them and then cops who were pretending they weren't cops. Typical cop show. I separated myself from the CISPES people, made certain I wasn't carrying anything sharp, anything illegal or anything political. I walked to a different gate, got patted down, searched and even asked my name. Then I walked in.

It was like being at a mall in any white suburb of America. No black people, no openly gay people, only a couple of rich Latinos and Asians, and no Native Americans. A band was playing Lee Greenwood's corny and even pathetic paean to patriotism. More than half the crowd was singing along— "God bless the USA…." The lead singer was a George Hamilton lookalike and the band was competent. The song still sucked. I wondered around feeling conspicuous with my long hair, beard and unpressed blue jeans. Most of the Reaganites ignored me like they did when they mistakenly ended up on Berkeley's Telegraph Avenue. It's like they figured if they don't look the weirdo in the eye, they won't be noticed. A small group of Reagan Youth (not the punk rock band) told me to get a job and cut my hair. I gave them the finger. Their alpha male guy responded in kind. We were even and went our separate ways. There was a GOP hack talking at the podium. I moved closer to an exit in case things got ugly. Ronnie Reagan was due to speak in less than thirty minutes. The anticipation in the crowd was building. It wasn't exactly the same as that last fifteen to thirty minutes before the Rolling Stones played the intro of their opening song, but the suits and hundred-dollar polo shirts were feeling it. Their great communicator was about to communicate. California Uber Alles. Meanwhile, my friends from the CISPES group had finally got into the stadium. They had somehow smuggled a banner reading US OUT OF EL SALVADOR into the venue and began to unfurl it. Within seconds, Reaganites from all sides attacked the small group and ripped the banner from their hands. Cops stepped in, reassured the Reaganites that the authorities would deal with the commies and that their leader would still appear on time.

Sure enough, ten or fifteen minutes later the song Hail to the Chief came over the tinny PA system and the stage began to fill up with people—mostly white and mostly ugly. The young Republican couple next to me could not contain their excitement. The male of the two squeezed his girlfriend closely and stuck his hand on the crotch of her Jordache jeans. I tried not to look and immediately heightened my senses. I could feel the threat from the folks around me. When the Star-Spangled Banner began playing over the sound system, I abandoned my normal response and stood up. It wasn't worth getting put in the hospital over a freaking song. After a couple fundraising pleas from the California GOP spokesman, Reagan shuffled to the stage. The teleprompter was turned on and he began his speech. It wasn't great communication. My favorite part was when he lost his place in the text rolling across the teleprompter screen because of some chanting from the few CISPES folks still in the crowd. I joined in of course. When he returned to his speech, it was clear to anyone listening that he had missed a sentence or two. Non-sequential words stumbled from his tongue. This form of addressing Republican crowds would become the norm in the years that followed, with each Bush taking this formless form to a different place and Donald Trump transcending them all in his incoherent ramblings that represent his speechmaking.

While Reagan caught up with his stumbling tongue cops in suits began to surround me. One such Robocop moved in next to me, flashed his badge and told me I needed to leave. I asked him why and he told me he didn't have to say. I asked him if he was arresting me. He told me if I left without any problem, I was free to go but I needed to go with his partner to the nearest exit. Being stuck between a cop and a hostile crowd, I nodded my head and followed the Secret Service suit out of the venue. Not wanting to stick around in the hope I would find my friends, I walked a mile or two, stuck out my thumb and hitchhiked to Santa Cruz, here the Reaganites were few and far between. At least in the places I hung out at.

The founding fathers were not that different than Donald Trump. They were slavers and believed the land they stole from the indigenous people was theirs by god-given right. The pursuit of profit informed what little conscience they had, just like it has informed most US presidents, if not all. History absolves them from very little, despite the mythology their successors have created around them.

The Boos at the Ballgame Were Just the Beginning, Mr. Trump

The cry of the mighty who are falling is growing louder. In the case of the USA it's a combination of angry accusations based on a confused bluster of humanity in the White House whose phalanx of fools exists so deep within its own perception of itself its members cannot conceive of their leader being booed at a national sporting event. Then again, neither can certain conservative pundits who do not like the man in the White House but slobber their servitude to its presence as some monument of integrity and honor. Honor in DC is a presumption I won't ever make, not even among those who are not thieves. I have more respect for the dope slingers and their customers, the hookers and their johns, and the panhandlers who sleep in places most of us never knew existed, than I do for the politicians and their paymasters. At least the former do a day's work and rarely misrepresent their intentions.

In other nations, the streets are consumed with protest against the failed leaders whose ill-gotten riches are failing to protect them from the wrath of those from whom they were stolen. In the grand imperial capital however, the masses are silent for reasons not apparent but all too clear. Too many gringos think they have something invested in that which steals their savings and their futures. They cheer the death of a villain from Iraq who never would have become the villain if they hadn't encouraged the military invasion and occupation that created him. There is no triumph in a human death, but the bloodthirsty insist otherwise. Those whose conscience is tied to the structure they exist in accept this manipulation of truth and cheer the death of a man whose demise means much less than the media would like us to believe. If the story is even true, that is. Fake news is not a new thing. It used to be called propaganda and we were told only the enemy would stoop to such methods. Of course, anyone with a critical mind unattached to the dogma of their particular State understands that all governments depend on propaganda to keep their populace informed in a manner that serves the ruling interests. Illiteracy is better, but misinformed literacy works equally well. It even provides an illusion of an informed populace.

This is a nation who considers the lousy actor and corporate shill Ronald Reagan to be one of its greatest leaders—the great communicator they call him. He was nothing but a racist shill with a withered peanut for a brain that confused television and the big screen with reality. The fact that Donald Trump, whose years as an asshole boss on the shaming exercise they call reality TV made him a household name in too many households across the United States, was elected president should surprise no one. The fact that he is losing his grip on both the office and his sanity reminds me of a Caligula reprise without the wine and togas. The sycophants he surrounds himself with are too self-involved to realize that riding on his train is not going to be the ticket to their version of heaven whether it's in the sky or their bank account. He's gonna' take a whole shitload of filthy fools who are going along with his con down with him. That is, unless the genuine fascists in his coterie start getting real serious and bring in their militias and fans in the military.

The spectacle known as politics in the United States has become more spectacular in an atrocious way these past few years. Once the impeachment show hits television, it is likely to become even more so. The histrionics from FOXNews and various MSDNC commentators are likely to make a certain amount of the procedure into a partisan debate about Trump, emphasizing that which makes them worship or abhor him. The key to the viewer is to keep the eyes on the prize—Donald Trump's departure from the White House and an exodus of his fascist and corrupt co-conspirators. Likewise, remember that those who expose his lies and abuses are not heroes, just players on a stage that demands they testify either as penitents or because they will go to jail if they don't. The real crimes are the ones no president ever gets impeached for.

The cynic in me—and there's a lot of that in me—questions whether the impeachment trial in the Senate will ever occur. The parameters of the inquiry are quite limited and reek of the imperial state—a state the Trumpists want for themselves, yet cannot seem to control their leader enough to make it their own. The idiotic and even stupid actions of Trump may do in that section of the capitalist class he claims to represent. The robber barons and their representatives in Congress and across the nation hitched their wagons to the Trump train and are now concerned he won't be able to bluster and lie his way out of this mess he's gotten them into. The fact that some of his most vocal supporters in Congress are dumber than a box of rocks does not help their cause. It seems a critical mass of stupidity may have been reached and the fact of Trump's departure before January 2021 may be realized. If so, the sinking ship that is this nation will not be righted but the captain and crew will be those who brought us to the Trumpist catastrophe in the first place—the neocons and the neoliberals. The warmongers and Wall Street thieves whose destruction of even the façade of a democratic republic created the cradle that birthed Trumpism and made overt racism and misogyny a way to win the White House again. The brash arrogance of Trump will return to Manhattan. The polished arrogance that kills foreigners with a smile and not a leer will return to the White House. The ghost of Richard Nixon's petty-minded impeachable self will be replaced with the ghost of Richard Nixon's grand and imperial self and Kissinger can die happy. I'll just be happy when he's dead.

There is a wild card in this prophecy, however. It is the phenomenon represented by Bernie Sanders' campaign. Although unlikely he will get past the numerous roadblocks and hastily constructed fences put up to keep candidates like him far from the seats of US power, there is the ever so slight possibility that his supporters' (who truly believe he can save this trash heap of a republic) optimism will sweep him into power. This is when this writer refers the reader to Bertram Gross's 1980s tract titled *Friendly Fascism*, wherein he describes in terms still relevant today how progressive candidates who talk seriously about redistributing the wealth downward instead of upward are blocked. If all else fails, he writes, the assassins will take up their positions, aim and shoot or poison or blow things up or well you get the picture. The monied classes like their money more than they like people, democracy, freedom and each other. That's why so many of them will put up with Trump's crassness and crudity. He puts more money in their pockets and makes it seem like the moral thing to do, as if there's anything really moral about accumulating wealth in the first place.

Many liberal and progressive pundits and their readers look into the nation's past for comparisons to today's situation. Of course, they exist: the 1920s, the gilded age of robber barons, Richard Nixon's final rise and fall. I suggest they look elsewhere if they want a more precise template that Trumpism fits into. That would be the Nazi rise to power in the 1930s. A quick look at that history reveals the manipulation of fears created by a defeat in war, economic insecurity and inequality, liberals unable and unwilling to accept that the nazis were not a normal electoral party, an electoral victory achieved without winning the majority of the votes and a ruthless verbal attack on the pre-existing bureaucratic establishment coinciding with a takeover of most bureaucratic functions by Nazi party functionaries. I can continue: a capitalist class at first uncertain and even opposed to Hitler and his party which eventually supported the party and its goals once they realized how much money they would make. It didn't take them long to realize that fascism was a great friend of monopoly capital and that its military and police apparatus would dispel those pesky people who believed in democracy. If Trump is not removed, the process his apparatus has begun could achieve a fascism that would put Hitler's to shame. Remember, you don't have to be Hitler to be a fascist. As for the neocons and neoliberals, remember that you don't need to be a fascist to be totalitarian.

The Failure of Bourgeois Law or, When the President Does It…It is Not Illegal

Trump is the Emperor who has no clothes. Since he was elected, his courtiers, the media and many residents of the United States have acted like the crowds in the classic fairy tale "The Emperor's New Clothes," going along with the charade that Trump is equal to his vanity or, at the least, not as bad as he originally seemed. His courtiers are more than willing to play his game as long as he cuts their taxes, locks up immigrants, and encourages white supremacists to run loose across the land. His detractors in power go on pretending, as well. After all, many of them are reaping the benefits of his tax cuts and, because he is so bad, they end up looking good. There are detractors, for sure, but they are from groups the powerful consider the usual discontents—intellectuals, students, leftists, Blacks, Latinos and a number of women.

Anybody expecting an investigation into the nature of the US presidency, the Congress or the foreign service was bound to be disappointed if they thought these impeachment proceedings would provide that. History tells us that presidential impeachments barely ever touch the secrets of the State. Even in the 1970s during the Nixon proceedings, it was the violations of campaign law by his re-election committee and the subsequent attempted cover-up of those violations that forced Nixon out of office. The revelations regarding FBI, CIA and NSA violations of the law and other criminal acts by forces of the state were only uncovered afterwards in hearings conducted by Senator Frank Church. Of course, it is unlikely the Church hearings would have occurred if the impeachment proceedings had never taken place. That being said, it is interesting to note that this particular impeachment is specifically focused on the way foreign policy is manipulated in the halls of power.

One of the observations from the Left—especially by those who saw no point in following the impeachment process—is that Trump was guilty of much greater abuses of power than attempted extortion in the Ukraine/Biden situation. Among those abuses are his ongoing abuse of immigrant families—specifically, children's separation from their parents and the use of the US military to police them. In addition, there were (and are) potential charges regarding his violation of the emoluments clause in the Constitution and the obstruction charges hailing from his stonewalling of both the Mueller and impeachment investigations. I've sat in a few courtrooms over the course of my life. Usually, this was because of my required presence after getting arrested at a protest or for possession of marijuana (back when it was illegal in every state in the union). One thing I noticed during the course of my courtroom watching was that prosecutors tend to take one of two approaches when charging defendants. They either throw the book at the person in the docket hoping one of the multitude of charges would stick, or they choose one charge to convict the defendant on. Often that charge was a misdemeanor instead of a potential felony. For example, a few years ago I was hit by a car.

I was in a crosswalk and had the right of way; the light was red but the driver drove right through the light, not slowing down even after striking myself and another pedestrian. The driver was charged with felony negligent driving with major injury resulting. The intent of the prosecutor was not to convict on the felony but to get the driver to plead to a misdemeanor charge. It worked. She pled to the lesser charge. It seems to this writer that the impeachment planners decided to focus on the singular charge of attempted extortion, knowing that other charges could end up in the final list of charges—among them obstruction of justice and lying to Congress.

While it was occurring, many people wonder what difference the process made. A big reason for this is that people accepted the framework provided by the mainstream media and the politicians. If one takes a step back and perceives it through a broader lens, it is apparent that the impeachment proceedings were part of a power struggle between factions of the capitalist class. The more they tear at each other; one hopes the more it delegitimizes their rule. Even though Trump was acquitted in the Senate, the impeachment matters, but not in the way the public is being told. It is their battlefield, but the public will pay the cost. If Trumpist fascism can be thrown from the White House in 2020, it seems that the nature of US politics would take a slight movement to the Left even if the Left does nothing. If Trump is still in the White House next February, chances are that much of the US population will feel the brunt of his lust for power. It is not likely to be pretty.

The story of the charges against Trump unfolded in front of the public like an intricately composed, albeit boringly presented, detective story. Given the stonewalling of the Trump administration, there were few smoking guns that the House committees could latch onto. However, there were enough that, when combined with the overwhelming circumstantial evidence, most intelligent viewers could see that there were impeachable offenses committed. In their ultimately pyrrhic battle to retain what little remains of the US republic and its approach to rule in a reasonably fair and democratic manner, the members of the House and Senate who voted for impeachment and removal of Trump from the White House have exposed its weakness when confronted with an executive branch that sees itself as something between a monarchy and a dictatorship.

There was serious bullying from the Trumpist forces during this process. Some House Democrats voted against impeachment because they were afraid of losing their seats in the fall 2020 elections. As far as I'm concerned, they deserve to lose them. The fact that this occurred, however, certainly adds fodder to the charge that the US electoral system and the political system it fills with small-minded and hollow humans is a pathetic joke. If the elections go the way they went in 2016—with Trump stealing the White House and Left-leaning Democrats shut out of their own party—even the façade of democracy will be gone, The Republic will have thrust the knife into its own heart the final time. Yes, there will be a government in Washington, but it will be a government that much of the rest of the world will likely see as the dictatorship (at least privately) it has been sliding towards for decades.

When Richard Nixon resigned in 1974, an argument could be made that the system worked. In other words, it removed a crooked executive. After all the histrionics, alarmist rhetoric and absurd comparisons of the Trump impeachment to the trial of Jesus Christ and other nonsensical analogies, what remains is the fact that because Trump remains in office the system did not work. One of the most corrupt and slimy humans to occupy the White House will remain in office, thinking he is vindicated and further destroying the already diminished presidency and the myth that is the United States. Donald Trump is the essence of US business and politics. He is the darkness that has always comprised a substantial part of the nation's soul. His continued presence in the White House makes it clear to all what really motivates the powerful in this nation. Far be it from me to mourn this turn of events except for the fact that it is the right wing and fascist elements that will reap the benefits (if that's what you call them) from the exposure of this truth.

Besides the reality that too many people think the impeachment means more than it does, too many citizens think they have no effect on politics. In essence, they have handed their power to the powerful. Like many other mechanisms of the state, impeachment is just a tool--it provides us with an opportunity to expose the nature of the system. It should not be an excuse to give up and act like we have no power. Instead, it should wake us up to the fact that our elected officials will only go so far in taking down one of their own, even one as openly crooked as Donald Trump.

I once wrote in regards to the resignation of Richard Nixon and his subsequent pardon by Gerald Ford that it was the pardon which proved how the system really worked. It works to protect its own. Nixon (and even Clinton) were at least somewhat ashamed of their actions once it became clear they would not get away with them. Donald Trump has no shame. The manipulation of the impeachment proceedings by his office and his supporters in Congress is not only what one calls peak arrogance, it has mocked the process and the legislature. In defense of the Trumpists, it is fair to say that Congress acceded to this mockery. By refusing to bring up charges regarding corruption and greater abuses of power, refusing to enforce its subpoenas, and by waiting as long as it did to even consider impeachment, the House of Representatives proved its greater interest lies with the pursuit of business as usual. Indeed, it's almost as if the fact of Donald Trump's abuses of their fractured system got in the way of their own pursuit of the power and monies Mr. Trump made his own. In the wake of Nixon's resignation and pardon, Jimmy Carter was elected. Carter's rhetoric promised a different United States; one of justice, honor and truth. As it turned out, within ten years the nation was ruled by a right-wing cabal with Ronald Reagan as its figurehead. The causes for his rule included cynicism on the part of the Left-leaning voters, rabid nationalism and racism on the part of the right, and a combination of numbness, self-deceit fostered by television, and self-centered greed on the part of those voters in between both political poles.

The story referred to earlier titled "The Emperor's New Clothes" ends with a parade where amid pomp and pageantry the Emperor shares his new and expensive outfit with his subjects. In what can best be described as the ultimate display of sycophantry, his courtiers, ladies, servants and subjects fill the air with remarks concerning the exquisite and beautiful nature of his new robes. Out of fear and the hope of some kind of reward, all who are gathered feed the Emperor's vanity by telling him and themselves bold-faced lies. Then, the child speaks up.

"'But he doesn't have anything on!" said a small child.

"Good Lord, let us hear the voice of an innocent child!" said the father, and whispered to another what the child had said.

"A small child said that he doesn't have anything on!"

Finally everyone was saying, "He doesn't have anything on!"

The emperor shuddered, for he knew that they were right, but he thought, "The procession must go on!" He carried himself even more proudly, and the chamberlains walked along behind carrying the train that wasn't there." -Hans Christian Andersen

This is where the United States stands in the year 2020. Not only is its leader a vain and narcissistic man, but an extraordinary number of his courtiers, advisers, generals and subjects feed his vanity, forsaking truth and honor in the name of their own greed and prejudices. Unlike the fairy tale, though, in this instance it will take more than the words of a child to expose the truth, if only because too many are too invested in maintaining the lie.

I held off on submitting this article until after Trump's State of the Union address and the Senate vote on the impeachment charges. The former is a misnomer and the latter was a fait accompli with Mitt Romney's vote to convict being the only surprise. One thing that was not present at Trump's speech was national unity and, as this piece states, the verdict in the Senate trial was never in doubt given the obstruction by the Trumpists running that body. The speech itself was typical Trump braggadocio based on lies celebrating the reactionary politics of the Trumpists and can be best summed up not in anything he said, but in the presentation of the Medal of Freedom to right-wing propagandist Rush Limbaugh.

Beyond Trump's vanity and arrogance is the very real possibility of fascism. The blind allegiance of his supporters in Congress and in the streets provides the essential element to any dictatorial regime. Trump and his financial backers have provided most of the rest. Over the course of the impeachment proceedings, two positions in the ruling class were made crystal clear. One position is beholden to bourgeois law. The other is beholden to Trump. Both are beholden to monopoly capitalism and the imperial policies it requires to continue its destructive ways. This was exemplified by the bipartisan applause the failed Venezuelan coup plotter Juan Guaidó received when he was introduced.

It cannot be stated enough, the victory of the Trumpist forces seems to predict a giant leap towards dictatorship. If nothing else, the Trumpists proved that if a powerful man openly flouts the law, he truly can get away with almost anything. The question remains: how far will this go? Will Trump order the invasion of Venezuela and perhaps Iran? Will his Department of Homeland Security intensify their racist and immoral attacks on immigrants? Will the Trumpists void future elections and just take over? Will the fact of a pliant Senate encourage Trump and his advisors to push through something akin to the Nazi law known familiarly as the Enabling Law, which made it possible for Hitler to enact legislation without the approval of the legislature? Will there be real resistance in the streets should such a scenario occur? The truth of Trump's acquittal by the Senate renders all of these possibilities more real than at any time since the US Civil War.

Don't laugh, don't cry, don't give up. Organize.

The Second Longest War in the United States

Other than the fact I was born in Minneapolis, I have little connection to the place. My adult life never encouraged much interaction with my relatives who live in the area, so except for the rare visit, I don't know much about it. However, I do understand police brutality and the nature of a police state. The current rebellion in the streets of the Twin Cities and around the United States—provoked by the blatant murder of a Black man by Minneapolis policeman who is also white and has a record of brutality—is a logical and emotional response to both.

The murdered man, George Floyd, was accused of trying to use a counterfeit twenty- dollar bill to purchase cigarettes. When confronted by a worker in the store where he made the transaction, Floyd apologized and gave pack the cigarettes. Then, the police showed up, put him in handcuffs, and proceeded to kill Floyd. Videos of the murder show a big man in a police uniform pressing his knee on the side of Floyd's neck for almost eight minutes until Floyd died. Despite the misleading reports that Floyd died later, the fact is that he was killed on that street by that cop. Three other cops did what cops usually do when one of theirs is engaged in brutal behavior—they blocked civilians from getting near the victim and threatened those who did come close demanding the policeman stop suffocating Floyd.

Now, I've unknowingly tried to pass counterfeit bills a few times at convenience stores when I lived in the Bay Area. Obviously, I'm not dead. Only once did the police get called. They asked me where I got the bill and let me go. Admittedly, this was back in the late 1970s and early 1980s, when things were supposedly different. However, the crucial difference is not what time period the incidents occurred, but the color of my skin and the color of Mr. Floyd's. The Minneapolis police know this and so do the rest of those who identify with the rulers in this country. This includes those politicians and officials who have spoken out against the police action. No one should be surprised at the rebellion in the streets. I doubt very many of the protesters are surprised at the reaction of the police to those protests. I know I'm not.

The tale behind the murder of Breonna Taylor is another too familiar representation of the US police state. Her murder from a fusillade of police bullets took place at the tawdry and often violent nexus where the never-ending war on drugs meets the US foundational racism. After another squad in the Louisville, Kentucky police department arrested an alleged drug dealer earlier in the day, another undercover police unit attacked Taylor's home under cover of the night. Taylor was murdered in the attack. Her friend, Kenneth Walker, fired his weapon in self-defense. There was never any reason for the police to go near Taylor's home and no drugs were found there. Although Walker was originally charged with attempted murder, no police have been charged, several weeks after the shooting. After public outcry from across the US, the charges were dropped against Walker. In my mind, Breonna Taylor was the victim of a drive-by shooting carried out by a gang of cops.

After trying to sweep the incident under the rug, various officials in Kentucky have taken minor actions against the cops involved because of public anger. That anger boiled over the night of May 28, 2020 when a protest turned violent. In fact, seven people were shot in the later hours of the protest. Police officials claim that no official police weapons were discharged at the scene. Given the current situation, that statement needs to be verified by objective sources. Although the public may never know, it seems quite possible that the shots were fired by white supremacists under cover of the night or by police provocateurs with unregistered weapons did.

Speaking of white supremacists shooting Black people, this trifecta of racist murders began with the murder of Ahmaud Arbery by three white supremacists in Georgia. This lynching in a development in small town Georgia would probably have gone unnoticed by the public if it weren't for the cellphone video taken by one of the murderers, Apparently, that video would never have gone beyond the local police department if one of the employees there had not leaked it. The three men charged are not merely garden-variety racists all too common in the USA. Instead, they are one pillowcase short of full-fledged Klan. The intent to murder is all too clear on the cellphone video. It will be interesting to see how their defense team wriggles out of a conviction. Yet I wouldn't be surprised if it did.

Likewise, I will not be surprised if the cops in Louisville and Minneapolis get away with these murders, despite the blatant nature of the crimes. Recent history tells us that there will be many twists and turns in the stories around these crimes. Some will be true and some will be false. Some will be published with the intent to confuse while others will be published with the intent to clarify. No matter what, the fact remains that these individuals were murdered by people who think they can get away with murder. Just like in war, very few murderers get convicted for their crimes and very few such crimes ever get reported. As for those politicians across the mainstream spectrum decrying the murders; unless they are ready to fundamentally change an economic and political system founded on the capture, trading and breeding of other human beings, they should be ignored. While police are certainly a big part of the problem, the system they are protecting is the fundamental problem.

I am not a Black man, but I certainly know there is a war against Black people in the USA. The only war that has gone on longer than this war is the one against the people who were here when the Europeans first arrived.

www.ingramcontent.com/pod-product-compliance
Lightning Source LLC
Chambersburg PA
CBHW051213250726
48655CB00006B/2391